Mountain Top Muse
Volume I

Mountain Top Musing
A Reluctant Poet's Glimpse
Into His Own Heart

Written By

Pete McKechnie

Design and Layout by

Nancy Smaroff

There will come a day
When my heart stops looking outside
And realize happiness lies within.
On that day, I will be happy.

Dedicated to

William, Peter and Luke

This book is for my sons. Until recently, they did not really know that I wrote, much less wrote poetry. I doubt they are old enough yet to even understand much of what I write. They most often witness me wielding a chain saw, or power tools. They have learned to ride dirt bikes, tractors. I have passed on to them a love of fishing, nature, playing in the mud. But more than any other thing, I want to show them how to be real men. I want them to understand that in order to be a real man, they first have to be real. And in order to be real, they have to follow their hearts. I want them to see that my heart expresses through poetry. I want them to understand that they will need to find whatever expresses most deeply within their own hearts.

Acknowledgements

I have many to thank for this project. Too many to list, as I am sure I will forget someone. To my family and friends who patiently pushed, and waited, commented and encouraged, until finally I decided that it was time to put my words into book for, I say thank you. I feel a deep sense of appreciation for your encouragement and patience.

There are two who deserve a shout out though. Tania DuBeau was instrumental in compiling my work. I have never seen myself as a writer, or a poet. I was just a man who happened to write poetry. I didn't write for the sake of writing, or for the sake of a career. I didn't write with the idea that my words might touch others, or be of value. That is what I thought writers did. I wrote mostly because the feeling to express something filled me, and writing was the outlet that seemed most able to satisfy that need. When Tania saw enough potential in my work to start compiling it without my knowledge, I started to understand that I am a writer and a poet. It was then I started to believe that perhaps the words that come to me and satisfy something in me that needs to express might, also, mean something to others.

A special thanks, also, to Nancy Smaroff, who started offering help, should I ever want to put my words into a book, almost a year ago. Her very quiet and gentle persistence allowed me the space to find within myself the willingness to accept her help.

So thanks to all of you who have encouraged me along this road, and I hope all of you know who you are. But thanks, especially, to Tania and Nancy.

With love…

Contents

Introduction

Life is the dance of the soul
Directed by the spirit
And lived by the heart.

There are times I write because of a specific experience, typically for me something that might happen outside. One such poem is 'Lessons From a Fledgling' which happened pretty much as written and led me to an understanding about myself. Sometimes it is an injustice, or justice, I hear about or witness, like 'Who Was The Angel?' Often, however, there is no clear inspiration for my poems. Often, while going about my normal routine, I simply realize that I have drifted into a space, almost like meditation, and it is time to express. There are times that something specific happened, and times that there was no occurrence. There are times a line or idea simply comes to me, and times when there is no starting point, just the feeling. At this point, I turn on some music, and it is very much as if what I write simply writes itself. A poem simply flows through me. I don't seem to be able to put myself in this state, and when it passes, I put my pen down, and don't try to force more to flow. Many years ago, a friend told me that I think with my heart. My writing feels like that to me, and the space I find myself in when I write feels like a point of connection that bypasses my brain and flows directly from my heart. From my heart to yours, I hope my words resonate.

A few years ago, I was having a discussion with a co-worker. She was having a particularly difficult time. After a short conversation, I suggested to her that she

leave work, and find a peaceful place to take a long walk. It was something that typically works for me when I feel challenged by life's trials, and since I was her boss, I felt good about giving her the time and space she needed to clear her head. Many hours later, after I had gotten home from work, I received a text with the following picture. I found it stunning, and immediately felt the desire to write. I didn't know what would come of it, but a handful of minutes later, 'Falling Into The River' had written itself. I have yet to visit that spot myself, and don't even know where it is.

Like water, time flows
Sculpting life like riverbanks
Cycles repeating

Winter settles in Silence
And solitude speaks
Spring's Awakening.

RISKING THE HEART

What would happen
If I offered my heart
Allowing myself the risk?

True, it could be hurt, rejected,
Tossed to the wind
Like the leaves.

But what would happen
If I held tight to my heart
Allowing myself no risk?

In truth, it would be hurt, rejected,
Tossed to the wind
By myself.

So, why not live
To offer my heart
Allowing myself the risk?

Holding strong to the faith
That tossing it to the wind
Is the act
That will give it wings.

GIFT OF THE SEASONS

Autumn's grip does not always come easy
For there is resistance
To the letting go
Which will lead to the darkness of winter.

Just as the colored leaves
Cling against the growing winds of change
In an effort to breathe once more
The heart will hold strong to the past
In an effort to justify
All that was previously felt.

It is the winter's caress
That is necessary,
And it will not always come easily.
It is only in the gift of letting go,
Allowing our branches to be blown bare,
Which allows the tender leaves of spring to grow.

In this letting go
Our hearts can both understand
The gifts of the past
And realize that to move forward in wholeness,
The dark winter days are the gift
That allows the offerings of spring to bloom.

PERSPECTIVE GUIDES

My truth lives within this moment—
Though I can resist this
Or accept it,
I cannot change it.

For it is the perspective I hold
As the moments of my life unfold
That guide my perception of my life.

There is no doubt
That I will have moments of joy
And moments of pain;
These are not within my power.

It is within my power
To relish the moments of joy,
With the understanding that joy
Is the nature of my life
Or to endure the nature of pain
Assuming that discord
Is the nature of my life.

I will see
That it is my choice
To allow each moment of joy
To be tainted by the truth of pain,
Or to allow each moment of pain
To be experienced
With the understanding
That joy is the nature of life.

EXPERIENCING THE MOMENT

Should one wish
To witness the reality of joy,
One only has to watch children
Whose explosion of laughter
Is unmitigated, unhindered
With thoughts of yesterday
Or tomorrow.
It is simply an expression
Of the moment
Of wonder
Unfolding in the present.

Should one wish
To experience the reality of joy,
One only has to be like a child
And explode in laughter
Unmitigated, unhindered
With thoughts of yesterday
Or tomorrow
To simply allow the expression
Of the moment to smile.

BECOMING

Life is not static. It is not something that happens.
It is a process of continual transition.
It is a process where we **were** what we were
Meant to be, **are** what we are meant to be,
And **becoming** what we are meant to become.

We may not have been always,
We may not be always,
But with each step of the journey,
We are what we are meant to **be**.

FALLING INTO THE RIVER

For centuries, the Stone has waited.
He has had his talk with the River
And now the time is right.
The Tree is close,
Roots exposed
Yet still firmly anchored along the River.
The Stone knows that soon
The Tree will look down
And understand.

"I understand," the Stone hears
On a cloudless spring day.
The Stone smiles and listens.
"Is that you great Tree," the River asks.
"Yes, it is I."
"And what is it you understand dear Tree?"

"I have spent my life digging in, holding on,
Burying my roots ever deeper
To resist your flow.
As I look down today
And see my massive roots exposed,
I understand just how strong
You have made me."

"You have grown strong, great Tree.
Do you understand what one day will happen?"
"Yes, dear River, now I understand.
Some day, I will fall into the loving arms
that created me."

"Yes, dear Tree, some day you will fall.
But not yet,
For you have no idea how strong you will become."

"Then, dear River, I can grow free from fear.
Now I understand
That what exposes me is love."

The Stone smiles, for he has known for centuries
That while his own path is slower
Some day he, too,
Will follow the River
To the Sea.

EMBRACING REALITY

Should I consider
The two greatest transitions
I will make in this life,
I will come to understand
That they are birth and death,
And that I have no choice
Other than to embrace
The reality of both.

For my ability to grasp
The reality of one
Determines my fate
To experience the other.

In the time
Between the transition of birth
And the transition of death,
I have a choice
To either foster the growth
Of my soul,
Or sit idly by
As time passes endlessly.

It is within these choices
That I will either
Allow my spirit to express
The eternal transformation of life,
Or keep it at bay
For fear of this expression.

While these choices
Can reflect the dramatic
Experience of birth
And incorporate the
Possible fears associated with death,

If the choice is not made
To experience the transitions
Possible in this life,
The process of birth and death
Will mean simply that I have not lived or died.

AFTER THE THAW

I sit,
Coffee in hand,
Staring aimlessly
Through the window
Into a crisp, late winter sky.

I notice the drip drip drip
Of an icicle
Hanging precariously from the eaves,
Winter's grip
Giving way to the warmth of the sun.

I begin to wonder,
Does it sense the loss
Of layers built through the frigid months?

Does it fear the stripping down to its elements,
Sense the mortality
Of a core it fears was never there?

Or does it carry the wisdom
No frozen heart can hold,
That after the thaw
It returns again
To the flowing, loving element
That is the sustenance
Of all creation?

THE RIVER, THE OCEAN

I can see
How the ocean might envy the River,
Honor the eternal flow
Across the land
To the shore.

I can see
How the river might envy the Ocean,
Honor the tremendous strength
Of the tides
Crashing against the shore.

Yet does the river fully understand
That its life feeds the ocean,
Or the ocean understand
That its life begins
Within the headwaters?

Does either fully see
That the shoreline is the illusion
And they are, in fact, One?

LESSONS FROM A FLEDGLING

I caught a bird today,
A fledgling, fleeing my presence
Unable to fly but a few feet at a time.

Holding it gently
Allowed it to escape,
So I caught it over and over again.

Its fear palpable through the flesh of my fingers,
Attempting to escape,
Not able to flee
Until exhaustion tempered its fear.

As I reached up towards its nest
In the eaves of my shed,
Its tiny fledgling claws dug deep into my fingers.
Holding on to what it most feared,
Holding on to what it must release,
And I found myself
Pausing to wonder,
What it is to which
I hold on?

LOST TREASURE

I can feel it is lost.
The nagging pull of emptiness
Too haunting to deny,
Still elusive is the object of my search.

Closet by closet,
Box by box
I search,
Diving into the basements of my past.
However, this thing I long for and miss
Remains hidden from my sight.

My past spreads out before me,
A confusing collage
Of all my hopes and dreams,
Mistakes made along the way,
Until the last box is emptied
And I see
A dusty frame
And I know it is
The answer to what I have lost.

I reach into the box.
I pick it up.
Dust it off.
And find myself looking into
A mirror.

THE PATH

For each of us
There is a path we walk.
Guided, misguided,
Found or lost,
It matters not,
For each of us
Takes up our path.

Some look forward
Believing they create the path,
While others feel lost along the way.
Both will look back one day and see,
That the path was actually given,
Not chosen,
And it brings us, ultimately, to ourselves.

SILENCE

It is often in silence
That the voice has the greatest depth.
For words can mislead,
Be misunderstood.

In silence,
The heart and soul can hear
Past the distraction
To the truth.

Therefore, I welcome the voice of silence,
As it often brings to me
The moments of
Greatest understanding.

WHO WAS THE ANGEL?

Late night road trip
Endless miles before and behind,
Diner lights calling
Along the empty road.
Lone waitress, tired
Pretty eyes darkened,
Pregnant belly swollen
Underneath her apron.

"Are you just slow,
Or are you stupid, too?"
I hear from a nearby booth.
"I told you I wanted more coffee."

She pours, and tries to smile.
Tries to still her shaking hand,
Ready for the next put-down.

Finally, she turns to me.
"I'm sorry," she says, guarded, ready.
"Yes, I can see you are busy," I say,
And she softens just a little.
"When you get the chance,
I would love a cup of coffee."

Back on the road
On the endless dark night,
I find myself wondering.
Who was the angel tonight?
Not I, for sure,
As I, too, have been that bitter old man
Having put my own frustrations
Before another's pain.

It was the waitress.
For it was she,
Through her struggles and pain,
Who offered me the chance
To feel compassion.

CONNECTION

Should we ever wonder
If a true connection
Might have been a mistake,
We will have to look deep
And understand
That connection
Is not an instance,
It is a state of being.
And should we not allow connection
Throughout our lives,
We will limit it
Within them.

By allowing ourselves
The grace to understand
That there is no mistake in connection,
We will understand
That if we do not embrace
The muddy waters
And connect with the souls
Who call to us,
We will ultimately destroy
Our own connection with ourselves.

AFTER THE STORMS

The downpours have passed,
For now,
And as the fog thickens
The faint glow of the moon
Appears through the thinning clouds.
I can hear
The beginnings of the nightly chorus.

While I know
That more squalls will surely come,
I bare witness
Through this nocturnal symphony
To my own ability
To awaken after the storms.

INTO DAWN'S LIGHT

As this night slowly
Fades into dawn
I understand
That there is joy
In this sadness
And peace
In this turbulence.

There is hope
In this despair,
And a level of comfort
In this pain,
Which can only be achieved
When I understand
That while I am here now
Soon, as always,
My dawn will come,
Bringing the loving gift
Of light
To my heart.

So I welcome this darkness
Not because it is real
Rather because without it
I cannot fully
Embrace the dawn.

SPEAKING THROUGH THE HEART

The heart does not express with intent,
It merely expresses.
And in its wholeness
Does not bother itself
With the interpretation of others.

It is the mind
Which expresses with intent,
And in its limited view
Fears the opinions of others,
Fears rejection,
And will speak untrue words
In order to gain acceptance.

I have the choice
To allow my heart to be slave to my mind
And speak half-truths
In the hope of being heard, accepted,
Or to allow my mind
To understand and accept
That what I truly want
Is to be seen exactly
As I am,
And the doorway to this reality
Is to give free reign
To my heart.

MY THREE SONS

What have I done to deserve this

I wonder

Listening to my inner voice

Loving endlessly

I count each blessing

And recognize each gift

My life has given to me.

Perhaps it is true that

Everyone is blessed in some way

That we all carry within us

Each other's hopes and dreams

Reaching endlessly toward fulfillment.

Living this life

Unfolding before my eyes

Kissing the fabric of my life with

Every breath I take.

This poem came on a New Year's Eve and started with the thought 'that would be a cool way to say New Year's Eve.'

HAPPY NEW YEAR

Honor the path this yeaR
As doorways open without agendA
Possibilities so diversE
Potential of the dawn's skY
Yearning incessantly to overfloW.
Nuance flows, blockages abdicatE
Eschewing yesterday's paiN
While opening joyouslY
Yielding on the doorsteP
Edifying spirit's workshoP
As old passes into A
Reality shifting toward spirit's oatH.

This poem came after a friend referred to the New Year's Eve poem as a double entendre. It was almost a challenge to myself after the idea popped into my mind. It took an hour or so, and almost crashed and burned a few times, but in the end that idea turned into Creation. I was not at all sure it was possible, but as is true for much of life, it's only impossible if you don't try.

CREATION

Creation Revolves Eternally, Ascending Towards
Infinite Oneness, Nothingness, Creation...

Reaching Endlessly, Always Timid, I Oblige,
Never Certain, Resolute...

Entering Another Transition, Intention Only,
Never Clear, Rarely Eager...

Attempting To Inspire, Obstinate Nagging
Crystalizes Repetitive Egoistic Attempts...

To Ignite Only Narcissism, Create Resentment,
Escapism, Absolute Turmoil...

In Oblivion, Nature Creates Rebirth, Eventually
Accepting The Initiation...

Opening, Natal, Centered, Reborn, Eagerly
Awaiting Timeless, Intimate Oneness...

Nothingness, Creation, Revolving Eternally, Ascending
Towards Infinite Oneness, Nothingness...

(First letter read down spells out the word creation.
First letter of each word, throughout the poem, read left to right spells out creation.)

MOMENTS

Life is lived in moments. We have the choice to spend these moments reliving the past or imagining the future. Neither of these is a negative choice, unless we allow ourselves to get caught up in the past, or enraptured by the future, to the extent that the moments we are given are lost.

To get lost in the past is to miss the possibility of creating another memory we might look back upon fondly at some point. To get too caught up in the future is to risk missing out on the fact that a future we dreamt of long ago is actually unfolding around us. While memories can be beautiful things, we can always, in this moment, remember them from the perspective of who we have become. And while dreams of the future can be wonderful, we can always be present enough to understand that, in this moment, we are already the dream.

I cannot both choose
To relish the moment I am in
And to cling to my perceptions
Of what my life should be.

For when I allow my experience
Of this moment to thrive
I cannot dwell on expectation,
And when I dwell on the perceptions
Of what I think I should be
I cannot be fully present
To the space I find myself in.

In truth my choice is simple.
I can live within the moment
And understand that I am always
Exactly where I am meant to be,
Or I can live with expectation
And know
That if all I ever see
Is what might become
I will never actually Be…

MATTERS OF PERCEPTION

Emptiness abides
Within the richest of worlds
For hearts who look to others
To still the fear
And change the course
Of a fruitless search for fulfillment.

Fullness abides
Within the darkest tribulations
For hearts who understand
That this seemingly fragmented world
Is merely mis-perception
Of a single loving God.

WHAT IF?

What if? I wonder.

What if there is a before
And an after,
A place where souls
Live their essence
And bathe in the light and love of God?

What if this life
Is nothing but a forge
That hones the heart
And inspires the soul
With the wisdom that all was created
In the image of God, of Love?

What if kindred spirits
On the eve of incarnation,
Realizing that chosen life paths
Would create the illusion of separation,
Could make a pact?
Could agree
That through the guise of coincidence
And the appearance of chance
They would touch base,
However briefly,
To hold just a little space?

Offering just a little support
And reminding each other
That, in some way,
We chose to live these trials, separately.

What if? I wonder.

AFTER THE DREAM

I lay awake, after the dream
Convincing myself in the darkness
That a dream indeed is what it was.

Minutes pass, many of them,
Before my heart slows, my breath calms
And I am lucid enough to know
That the nightmare was not so real,
That all is well, all is light.

As I walk my way back towards slumber
In the middle of this night,
I find myself wondering, for a moment
If that is how an angel feels
As it awakens from a life.

ALLOW

If it is not I .
Who allows myself to love,
Then who is it
That gives me this gift?

If it is not I
Who allows myself to see,
Then who is it
That opens my eyes to sight?

If it is not I
Who allows myself to feel,
Then who is it
That guides my heart?

It is I, of course,
Who allows myself to love,
Who allows my visions to be seen
And my feelings
To guide my heart.

Therefore, it is not
That I am allowed to live this life.
It is simply
That it is I
Who allows myself to live it.

POWER OF WORDS

It is both said
That God spoke
This world into existence
And that we are created
In the image of God.

I wonder how it can be, then,
That we do not seem to understand
That the words we speak
Will create our reality
And the words we don't
Will limit it?

EXPERIENCING GOD EXPERIENCING

What if my life were merely
An experience had by God?
Would gratitude be easier to find
When my days were brightened by the sun?

Would I understand
That it was not me experiencing joy,
Rather it was God finding joy
In the experience of my creation?

Would I find,
In the trials I face or
In the agony of others,
An understanding that they are all God's?

That it is God's way
To gather the seeds
Which sow forgiveness and compassion?

What if my life were merely
An experience had by God?

For what could I be
More thankful?

LIES ABOUT MYSELF

It is not the lies
That others might speak of me
That bring turmoil
To my heart.

Rather it is the lies
I might speak of myself
Which carry the true weight.

When I claim to myself
That I am unworthy
My heart will never understand its worth.
When I claim to myself
That I am unloved
My heart will never feel
The love of creation shining down upon me.

When I claim to myself
That I am better than, or worse,
The very words form a barrier
To connection with others.
When I claim to myself
To be either more than, or less,
I deny the very nature of oneness,
The reality that we
Are not only all one,
But that we are all the same.

So, while the lies spoken by others
Might feel like arrows
Piercing my soul,
It is in fact
The lies I might speak of myself
Which create the walls
Between the true nature of my heart
And myself.

REFLECTIONS OF MYSELF

'Tis not the beauty of others
That I witness
When I look into their eyes,
Rather the reflection of myself in them.
And should I vow
That I will never gain their embrace,
It is merely that I feel unworthy
Of being beautiful.

'Tis not the strength of the oak
That I witness
As I watch the boughs bend with the wind,
Rather the reflection of myself in them.
And should I vow
That I could never withstand the gales,
It is merely that I feel unworthy
Of its strength.

'Tis not the power of the ocean
That I witness
When I stand upon the shore,
Rather the reflection of myself in it.
And should I vow
That I could never carry that force,
It is merely that I feel unworthy
Of holding such power.

So, 'tis not reality
That I witness
When I look out upon the world,
Rather the reflection of myself in it.
And should I vow
To open my heart,
I will understand
That what I see most clearly in the world,
I will ultimately see most clearly
In myself.

THE NATURE OF BEING WORTHY

To allow myself to think
That there is something I have to offer,
That my presence can
Somehow be a gift to this world,
I must also think
I have worth,
I must think that the world
Will be a better place
For my life.

And what risk is there with this thought,
Other than the understanding
That all souls can say the same?
So should I accept
That my path has worth
I have little choice,
I must understand
That the paths of all others
Are guided by the same light
That gives worth to mine.

SILENCE

It is tempting to believe
That those with the
Greatest ability
To weave words together
Are those whose gift
Of communication is best.

But words can be chosen,
asked not only to follow
But also to guide an agenda,
Thus becoming not so much
Communication
As propaganda.

Perhaps we should understand
That it is in silence,
Pure presence,
That the greatest communications
Will occur.

For without words
To get in the way,
The heart and soul
Can truly speak.

BLESSINGS OF FAITH

Faith is not the ability
To believe
That somehow everything
Will work out fine.

It is the understanding
That in this very moment
I am where,
And what,
I am meant to be.

Faith is not the notion
That someday, God will bless my life.
It is the knowing
That in this moment,
I am blessed.
That in this moment
God is smiling on me.

All I have to do
Is understand
That all that is given to me
Are these moments,
And should I not embrace them all
I will miss out on that with which God
Wishes to bless me.

THREE RIVERS

While it might seem as if
  The heart
    The mind
      The soul
Flow like three divergent rivers,
Each in motion
Yet at odds with each other.

It is with time
  And Hindsight
    That we will see
Each of these rivers flows
To the bay, the sea
And ultimately, the ocean.

While their journeys
Might seem divergent,
Ultimately
  All three
    Will meet
      In the truth
        Of their oneness.

COMMUNE

It is within our fumbled words
That communication most often fails.
Words cannot carry
The energy,
The intent,
Of the soul.
And the heart cannot express
In mere words
The depths that lie within.

Should we learn to communicate
With each other
As the blossom speaks with the bee,
As the river communes with the mountain valleys,
As the Earth guides the migration of the herds,
Then we will find
We all seek the same thing,
Long for the same expression,
And hold within us the power
To truly commune.

PERCEPTION THROUGH THE FOG

Circumstance
Might seem to be
The guiding force of life,
It is perception
That creates the flow.

Circumstance
Might be seen as out of our control.
It is the perception
Of that circumstance
Which holds the key
And unlocks the door,
To either misery
Or joy.

So while it is tempting
To perseverate on circumstance,
It is far more productive
To alter our perception,
And to realize that our lives
Are nothing more,
Nor less,
Than we perceive.

STILLNESS

Into the stillness
Of the snow-carpeted forest
I walk,
And notice
That there is nothing to see,
No distraction,
No action;
Just the silent beauty
Of the Now.

As I ponder this silence
On this crisp winter's day,
I begin to understand
That I can more easily quiet myself,
More easily connect into this world,
When the distractions
Of activity
Are silenced, hidden.
And the awareness I sense
With nothing outward
On which to focus
Is directed inward, instead
To my Heart.

THE DANCE OF DARK AND LIGHT

In these moments before dawn
As light begins to brighten the sky,
It is easy to feel
That it is the morning's light I crave.
And as I try to sit silent
Being present in this moment
I long to believe it is the light I need.

In these moments before dawn
When I allow the silent darkness to abide,
I begin to understand
That it is the transition from darkness I crave.
And should I sit silent
Being present to this darkness
It will lead me more easily to the light.

So, in these moments before dawn
As darkness and light dance in the sky,
I will allow myself to understand
That I crave both darkness and light.
And when I sit silent
Being present to the gift of both,
I will understand that the darkness and light are one.

DREAMERS

To live in this moment
Is still to live in this world,
To experience
The sensation
Of tactile wonder,
To live fully a life
In this reality.

To live in the space
Between each moment
Is to understand,
That what is experienced
In the moment
Is the dream,
And the one who
Experiences it
Is the dreamer.

In the sporadic moments
Of awakening
We see
That it is not
That we awaken
From a dream,
Rather, we awaken
To the understanding
That we are
the dreamer.

WITNESSING THE GIFT

I awaken at dawn, alone,
To face this day
And I ask myself
What shall I do with it?

I can choose
To embrace this day
For what it has to offer
Or lament it
For what it does not.
Either way, the day
Will be what it is.

So with each dawn
There is the danger
That I will fail
To see the gift,
But also the possibility
That I will embrace it,
Whatever gift might come to be
With this dawn.

LOVE, AND LOVING

We reserve certain words
For those held most dear,
While at times
The world passes by
Unnoticed.

I can say
I love you,
Within a certain context
But can I say
I love you
To my life,
Can I simply say
I love?

I will hope that I can do both.
That I can gaze into my lover's eyes
And say I love you,
And that I can witness my life
And say I love.

The challenge might be
To see that one
Does not depend
On the other,
But that both,
Together,
Are what this life
Inspires.

WHAT MATTERS?

It matters not
That others might tell me
It is safe to jump from this cliff.

It matters not
That my eyes
Should witness their leaps.

For the ears,
The eyes,
Both speak to the mind,
And make no mistake,
It is the mind
That fears the fall.

It matters, however,
That my spirit might guide me
To this cliff.
And it matters
That my heart
Can witness the leap.

Because the spirit and the heart
Speak directly to the soul,
And it is the soul
Which relishes the flight.

ALLOWING THE COLLAPSE

There are moments
In which I feel lost,
When I can see my world
Crumbling around me,
Collapsing.

In these moments
I have a simple choice.

I can choose to believe
That all which I think I know
Has shifted, is about to collapse,
Or choose to understand
That what collapses
Beneath my feet
Is the shield I place
Between my reality
And my truth.

CREATION'S LOVE

As I walk through this forest
I see the act
Of creation's love.

I see how strong the love of the soil
Is for the trees
As it holds the roots tight
Against the winds.

I witness the power of love
As the banks of the stream
Hold the flowing water.

I feel the power of creation
In the hummingbird's dance
Within the petals,
And the subtle show of strength
The tender shoot exhibits
As it emerges from the soil.

And I witness, understand
That it is the nature of life
To Love,
To Create,
To Grow.

MAKING LOVE TO LIFE

We have a limited view
Of love.
When we consider
Making love
We think only
Of a partner, a lover,
A dance in which we share another's body.

To make love, truly
Is to make love with life,
To understand
That the greatest desire
Is to feel the connection
With reality,
That we feel when
We are deeply connected
To a lover.

So let me make love
Not only with a lover
But with my life,
Let me know
The depth of joy which comes
In a lover's arms.

Let me grasp
The depth of understanding
That will come
Only when I love my life
With the same intensity
With which I love my lover.

UNFOLDING ALLOWED

When I look back, someday,
On my life,
On this moment,
I will know that I have loved.
I will understand
That the nature of pure connection
May not play out
As my mind might hope
Nonetheless will always
Feed the heart and soul,
And provide the sustenance
For a life well-lived.

Knowing this,
Though I may not know
Where this love will go,
I find my self
With little choice
But to fall headlong into it,
And allow my heart to open
To that which I don't understand
And to allow my heart to fly
Into unknown winds.

BE HERE NOW!

If I allow myself to wonder
Where I would want to be right now,
I will have to understand
That I am not
Where I need to be.

For as the bright yellow flower
Of the dandelion
Does not wonder
What the seed-head feels,
The seed-head
Does not lament
The passing of the flower.

So I should not wonder
What might become of me,
Or dwell on what I was before.
I should merely find within myself
The ability
To be here now,
As I am.

IF NOT ME, WHO?

Who am I to think
That I could change the world?

I laugh at myself,
At the thought.
I allow the notion
That there is nothing
I could ever do
To affect change on that scale
To pass through my mind.

Then I wonder
What would happen
If all of us
Allowed this powerlessness
To define our lives?

I begin to understand
That while it is not within my power
Or up to me
To change the world,
It is within my power
And up to me
To change myself.

And if I become one of many
Who open to this understanding,
Together we will indeed
Change the world,
And together
We will create
A world worthy
Of passing on to our children.

WHICH LIFE WOULD I CHOOSE?

I could choose
To clothe myself
Or to expose myself.

I could choose
To layer myself
With the expectations
Of the world,
Like a coating of make-up
Designed to hide
My true self,
Or I could choose
To lay myself bare,
Unadorned, real.

One choice
Might garner acceptance,
And with the right costume
Could even guarantee
A life of ease.
While the other
Could garner understanding,
And with no costume
Could even secure
A life of love.

THE VOICE OF THE SOUL

There are times
I find myself
Without words, ideas.
When I allow
Those times
To offer direction
To my heart,
I understand
That this is when
I can most clearly
Express the voice of my soul.

EACH THREAD IS GOLDEN

We would think no less
Of the thread
Who in the hands of the weaver
Could not fully understand
Its place
In the fabric.

We would see,
Simply,
The whole;
Appreciating the woven art.

Why is it,
That in order for us
To feel whole,
We somehow need
To understand our place?

Why is it we cannot
Understand
That our place
Is simply to be ourselves
In this grand fabric
Reality weaves?

Why does it have to
Be so difficult
Just to take our place
And be?

A LOVING EARTH

I feel the breeze
Against my skin,
The heat of the sun
Caressing my shoulders.

I feel the leaves
Beneath my feet,
The forest floor moist,
  Accepting,
    Welcoming.

I witness the treetop dance
Of the squirrel,
Hear the distant call
Of the hawk, unseen,
Flying somewhere
In the brilliant sky.

The deep, earthy smell
Of the forest
  Mingles,
    Combines,
      Coalesces,
With the scent of wildflowers.

And when I open to this,
I know,
That each step
Through this wilderness
Brings the opportunity
  For the Earth
    To make love to
      My senses.

FOLLOWING MY PATH

Listen to me
If you choose,
Learn from me
If you can,
But do not follow me.

Do not walk behind me
Down my path.
Doing so
Will guarantee only
That you are not
Following your own.

So listen, learn.
Walk along beside me
Until our paths diverge.
Because each of us
Leads the way
Down a path that is empty
Behind us,
Yet intertwined
With all souls whose paths
Keep us pointed
Towards our own.

THOUGHTS ON GRATITUDE

I can say thanks,
I can express gratitude
In the moment
And do my best
To always do so.

This is easy,
And at times I find myself
Wanting more to know
How to truly live in gratitude,
And express it within
Every breath
That I am given.

There are times
I want to express gratitude,
Not in this moment
But in this life.
There are times I understand
That it is my life
I am grateful for,
And that all those who pass through it
Allow me to live it
As I am meant to do.

In these times
I understand
That I should be grateful for everything,
Every experience,
Every moment,
Whether they
Bring pain or joy,
Understanding that without them all
I will never become
The being I am meant to be.

NO LONELINESS IN SOLITUDE

While they may seem similar,
There is a difference,
A distinction,
Between solitude and loneliness.

One, solitude,
Is a state of being.
While the other, loneliness,
Is a state of mind.

One, solitude,
Allows us the time
It takes
To understand
That while we are distinct,
We are also connected.

The other, loneliness,
Fosters the illusion
That connection
Is not the natural
State of being.

In truth,
Solitude opens us
To the understanding
That we are simply
A strand in the web,
While loneliness closes us
To the understanding
That we are fundamentally
Connected to everything.

LOVING AND GIVING

I find myself disinterested
In peace, or comfort, or joy.

I find myself disinterested
In a life of ease,
A life without disharmony
Or the waves of discord.

I find the life I desire
To be a life of love,
Perhaps the most challenging course.

For a life of love
Does not promise or rule out
Peace, comfort, or joy.
It does not promise ease.

But a life of love gives,
And if I could hope greater
Than to give,
Even if my own life
Seems full of discord,
I don't understand
What hope is for.

RICHES OF SPIRIT

I could attain
Riches beyond belief
In this life time.

I could gather wealth
Beyond reason,
And swim in pools
Of gold.

I could, also, choose
To let go
Of wealth and gold.

I could choose, rather,
To listen to
The quiet voice
Of my heart,
Which may not
Resonate clearly
With the path of wealth,
But has no choice
But to resonate
With the path
Of my spirit.

PAGE BY PAGE

Let me read my life,
Page by page,
In the way
I would read the most interesting story.

Not caring, really,
What each page
Might hold,
But simply
Diving into the reality
Each page weaves
As I delve into the mystery
That is the story.

Let me not worry
About the past
Or fret for the future,
Rather allow me the gift
Of experiencing only
The page I am reading.

Let me read my life
With pages already read
Holding no more weight
Than the pages yet to come,
With the words
I am currently reading
Speaking volumes
To my spirit
As it presents itself,
Right now.

THE OAK

There is great strength
In the Oak
As it stands
In the stillness of a summer's day,
Near motionless, resolute…

Yet in this strength
Perhaps there is a weakness,
Because there is no chance
Of mobility
In this valiant
Show of fortitude…

Now add the storms of summer
As the winds churn
With their own true strength,
And the mighty Oak,
Once silent,
Begins to dance…

Now is when the true power
Of the Oak
Can be witnessed.
And while it might
Ultimately crash to the ground,
It will come to understand, first,
The mettle from which it is made…

So let me not stand
Strong and resolute,
In the stillness of a summer's day.
Rather let me find
The true nature of my Soul
In the storms
That might ultimately destroy me.

For while the stillness
Might describe me,
It is the tempest
Which will define me…

FAMILY

Offer me a definition
Of family,
And explain to me
What this word means.
Tell me it means my blood,
And I would agree.

Add my friends
And with a full heart
I would nod and smile.
But suggest
That family
Ends here
With family and friends,
And I would disagree.

Suggest to me
That family
Does not include
The forest
In which I live,
Or the myriad of creatures
Which live within it.

Suggest to me
That family
Does not include
The balance of humanity
Which might not
See the world
In the ways
That I do,

Or the infinite universe
Which might not even
Have the grace
To notice my being.

Do this and I will suggest
That you
Perceive too small a world,
And you
Do not fully understand
The fullness possible
With the notion of
Family.

THE GRANDEST OF YOUR CREATIONS

Dear Creator,
Allow me narcissism.
Allow me the grace
To see myself
As the grandest
Of your creations.
Allow me an ego
Capable
Of seeing myself
In such a grand light.

Dear Creator,
Allow me humility.
Allow me the grace
To understand
That of all your creations,
My ego is but one of many
And while mine
Might be a grand light,
All others shine
As brightly.

Dear creator,
Let me understand
That your creation
Is not only me,
It is everything.
And if I should
See value
In myself,
I would
See the beauty
And value
In it all.

ABOUT THE AUTHOR

Pete McKechnie

Poet and carpenter, woodsman and mystic, Pete is a man of few words. He has learned that silence allows the space to listen, and listening allows the spoken word to flow without agenda. This understanding came while teaching meditation classes and facilitating Vision Quest.

Now, his writing has become a form of meditation, inspired often by listening in silence to the world around him, and his words capture the connection that comes when we silence ourselves and just witness the voices of the world around us.

Contact Pete at:

mountaintopmuse@gmail.com

Or visit him on FaceBook:

Mountain Top Muse

Made in the USA
Middletown, DE
26 August 2018